MONEY MATTERS

young

Entrepreneurs

Addition and Subtraction

Kristy Stark, M.A.Ed.

Consultants

Michele Ogden, Ed.D
Principal
Irvine Unified School District

Colleen Pollitt, M.A.Ed.
Math Support Teacher
Howard County Public Schools

Publishing Credits

Rachelle Cracchiolo, M.S.Ed., *Publisher*
Conni Medina, M.A.Ed., *Managing Editor*
Dona Herweck Rice, *Series Developer*
Emily R. Smith, M.A.Ed., *Series Developer*
Diana Kenney, M.A.Ed., NBCT, *Content Director*
Stacy Monsman, M.A., *Editor*
Kevin Panter, *Graphic Designer*

Image Credits: Cover, pp.1, 8 AP Photo/Austin American-Statesman www.statesman.com, Rodolfo Gonzalez; p.9 (front) Patrick Ecclesine/© ABC/Getty Images, (back) Michael Desmond/ABC via Getty Images; p.10 Charles Sykes/AP Images for Microsoft; p.11 Saul Loeb/AFP/Getty Images; p.12 Kent State University; p.14 age fotostock/Alamy Stock Photo; pp.16, 19 Courtesy of Asya Gonzalez, Stinky Feet Gurlz www.stinkyfeetgurlz.com; pp.20, 25, 31 Courtesy of Moziah Bridges; p.22 Michael Ansell/© ABC/Getty Images; p.23 Giovanni Rufino/© ABC/Getty Images; all other images from iStock and/or Shutterstock.

References Cited: Kim, Larry. 2014. "This 12-Year-Old CEO Runs a $150,000 Business." Inc.com. http://www.inc.com/larry-kim/this-12-year-old-ceo-runs-a-150k-business.html.

Teacher Created Materials
5301 Oceanus Drive
Huntington Beach, CA 92649-1030
http://www.tcmpub.com

ISBN 978-1-4258-5547-5
© 2018 Teacher Created Materials, Inc.

Table of Contents

What Is an Entrepreneur?

You are probably asked this question a lot: *What do you want to be when you grow up?* Some people want to be doctors. Some want to be astronauts. Others want to be engineers or professional athletes. It can be hard to choose from so many jobs!

Some people want to start their own businesses. They are called **entrepreneurs** (on-truh-pruh-NURS). When a person owns a business, he or she is the boss. The boss gets to make all of the important decisions about the company.

Owning a business is not just about making decisions. It means the person in charge has to do a lot of work, too. When they first start, business owners often have to do everything by themselves. They might have to wait until they are **successful** to hire **employees**.

At any stage, though, entrepreneurs have a tough job. They must know how to deal with problems and persevere in solving them. But, they are passionate about what they do and embrace the challenges!

food truck owner

general contractor

small-business owner

OPEN

Entrepreneurs have to be **creative**. They imagine things that can make the world a better place. Most people start by thinking of something they are good at or something they love to do.

A florist arranges a bouquet of flowers.

6

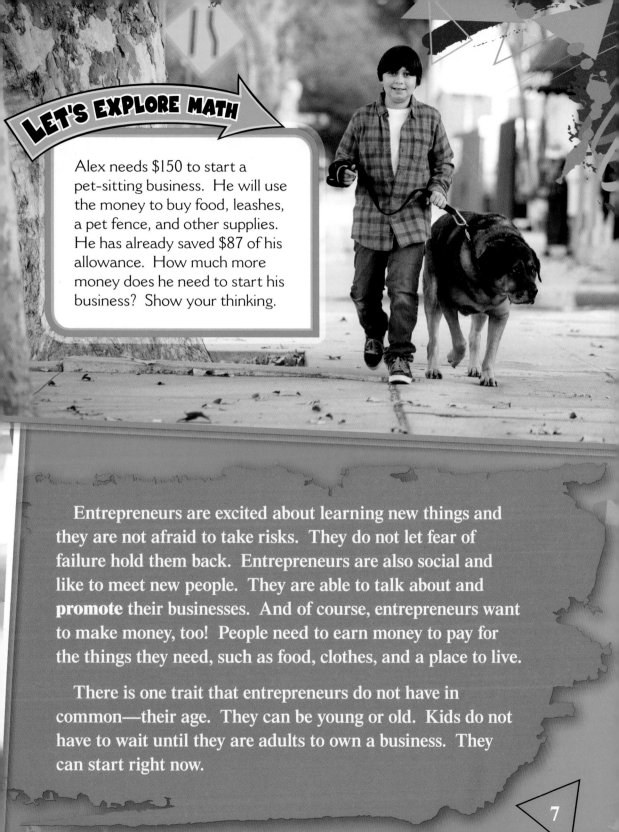

Alex needs $150 to start a pet-sitting business. He will use the money to buy food, leashes, a pet fence, and other supplies. He has already saved $87 of his allowance. How much more money does he need to start his business? Show your thinking.

Entrepreneurs are excited about learning new things and they are not afraid to take risks. They do not let fear of failure hold them back. Entrepreneurs are also social and like to meet new people. They are able to talk about and **promote** their businesses. And of course, entrepreneurs want to make money, too! People need to earn money to pay for the things they need, such as food, clothes, and a place to live.

There is one trait that entrepreneurs do not have in common—their age. They can be young or old. Kids do not have to wait until they are adults to own a business. They can start right now.

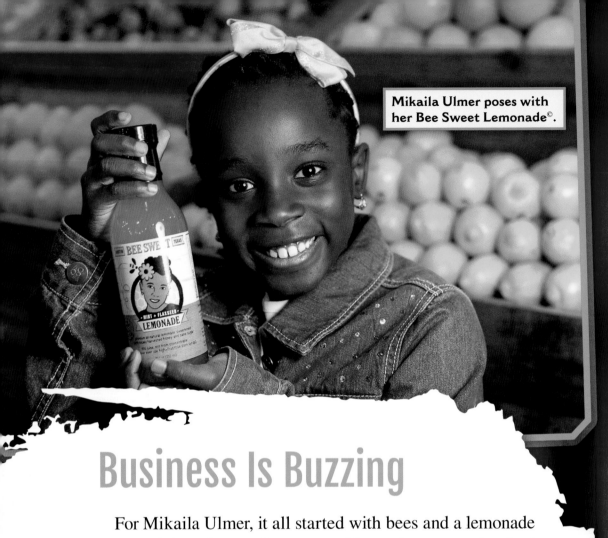

Mikaila Ulmer poses with her Bee Sweet Lemonade©.

Business Is Buzzing

For Mikaila Ulmer, it all started with bees and a lemonade recipe. When she was four years old, two bees stung her in the same week! That painful experience made her want to learn more about honeybees. She learned that they are dying and could soon become **extinct**. Ulmer wanted to help. She learned that using honey from local beekeepers supports the bee population and helps it grow. So, she decided to make a lemonade recipe from her great-grandmother. And she used honey to sweeten the drink.

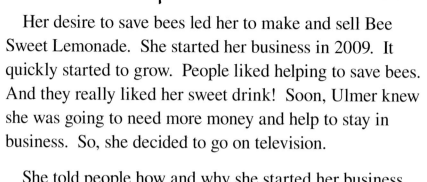

Her desire to save bees led her to make and sell Bee Sweet Lemonade. She started her business in 2009. It quickly started to grow. People liked helping to save bees. And they really liked her sweet drink! Soon, Ulmer knew she was going to need more money and help to stay in business. So, she decided to go on television.

She told people how and why she started her business. She asked them to **invest** money. A man named Daymond John said he would give her $60,000 to grow her business.

Ulmer and her dad appear on a show called *Shark Tank*.

Daymond John

Since John's investment, Ulmer's drink has been renamed Me & the Bees Lemonade©. She also signed a huge deal with Whole Foods Markets®. Her drink is now sold in over 50 stores. A company called United Natural Foods, Inc. (UNFI) sells her lemonade, too.

For Ulmer, it's not about money. She remembers her goal to help save bees. She gives part of her **profits** to groups that help protect bees. She also teaches workshops to help people learn how to save honeybees.

Mikaila Ulmer presents her company at a student showcase in New York.

Ulmer has stayed busy. She has received many awards for her work. In 2015, she went to the White House Kids' State Dinner. She got to meet and talk with President Barack Obama. She even served him a glass of her lemonade.

Ulmer isn't busy all the time, though. Her mom makes sure she takes breaks from work. She spends time doing other activities, like in-line skating and hanging out with her friends. She also likes to sleep over at her friend's house. Time with friends can lead to business talk. She enjoys helping her friends start their own businesses.

LET'S EXPLORE MATH

Ulmer needs to calculate her profits for April.

Revenue – Expenses = Profit

Suppose her business generates $14,958 in **revenue** during the month. Of this amount, $8,234 is spent on **expenses**. What is the profit? Explain how you can check your answer to be sure it is correct.

Ulmer meets President Obama at the United State of Women Summit in Washington, DC.

Strong Business "Scents"

Richard "Hart" Main's business started out as a joke. In 2010, his sister Camryn was selling candles for a school fundraiser. Thirteen-year-old Main laughed at the "girly" scented candles. He told his mom and sister that someone should make candles for guys. His mom didn't laugh. Instead, she encouraged him to make candles with scents that appealed to him. That's just what he did!

Richard "Hart" Main poses with his ManCan candles.

Main named his company ManCans. He began with the $100 he had in his **savings** account. His parents also gave him a $200 loan. He used the money to buy candle supplies and soup. Why did he need soup? Main did not want to put his "manly" candles into glass jars. He wanted his candles to look different, in addition to smelling different. So, he poured his candles into the empty soup cans.

Main's business started to grow. ManCans started with eight candle scents, including bacon, campfire, and sawdust. He now has 17 candle scents! Over the years, he has had to make some changes to keep up with this growth.

A volunteer pours soup at a soup kitchen.

Main's friends and family could not eat enough soup to get the cans needed to fulfill orders. So, he began donating soup to a soup kitchen near his home. The soup kitchen was able to feed people who could not afford to buy their own food. Then, they gave the empty cans back to Main. Main was able to make even more candles.

Today, ManCans donates money instead of soup. Seventy-five cents from every candle goes straight to local soup kitchens. This is Main's way of helping others.

Suppose that Main donates $1,478 in March and $3,765 in April to a local soup kitchen. Use the number line to answer the questions.

$0 $1,000 $2,000 $3,000 $4,000 $5,000 $6,000

1. Round $1,478 to the nearest thousand dollars. Use the number line to justify your answer.

2. Round $3,765 to the nearest thousand dollars. Use the number line to justify your answer.

3. Use your rounded answers from questions 1 and 2 to find the total estimated amount of money donated in March and April. Do you think your estimate is greater than or less than the exact total? Why?

Main and his mom used to make candles in their home. But ManCans grew fast. First, they rented space and hired a few employees to help. But, they still couldn't keep up. So, he hired the Beaver Creek Candle Company. This company now makes and ships his candles. But, Main still oversees the process.

Main's success keeps him busy. In 2015, he was named Young Entrepreneur of the Year from the National Federation of Independent Business (NFIB). He also wrote a book called *One Candle, One Meal*. Main now studies **economics** at Kent State University.

Asya Gonzalez poses with her Stinky Feet Gurlz T-shirt.

A "Gurlz" Business

Asya (AY-zhuh) Gonzalez has big dreams of becoming a fashion designer. So, when her mom showed her a picture of a woman's face that she had drawn when she was a kid, she was inspired. Gonzalez tweaked her mom's drawing a bit. Her mom loved it! She decided to combine the two things she was best at—drawing and fashion. Gonzalez designed T-shirts with her doodles on them. At fourteen years old, she had become an entrepreneur.

Gonzalez knew she would need help to get her business up and running. Luckily, her parents were able to give her ideas and **resources**. They also helped with the **finances**. Her mom gave her the idea for the name of her company. She said that when Gonzalez was little, she and her cousin used to run outside a lot. When they came inside and took off their shoes, their feet smelled bad. Gonzalez's grandma teased them for having "stinky feet." Just like that, she knew what she wanted to name her company. Stinky Feet Gurlz© was born!

LET'S EXPLORE MATH

Imagine that for the month of December, Gonzalez's revenue is $2,675 and her profit is $1,088.

Revenue − Expenses = Profit

What are her expenses for this month? What strategies did you use to find the solution?

As her company started to grow, she knew she wanted to help others. So, the same year she started Stinky Feet Gurlz, she also founded a charity. She Is Worth It! works to stop slavery of girls around the world. A portion of her profits goes to this charity. Gonzalez hopes she can help keep girls safe.

Gonzalez helps people in other ways, too. She serves as a **mentor** to other young entrepreneurs. She helps them start businesses the same way that her mom and dad helped her. She hopes she can inspire other teenagers to pursue their business ideas, too.

In 2015, she won the Dan Danner Leadership Award from NFIB. It is given to support young business owners. She won her award from NFIB the same year as Main!

Gonzalez was once asked what she has learned from her business. She said that she has learned how to be a leader in her community.

Asya Gonzalez co-hosts *Express Yourself!*, a teen radio program.

Mo Bridges poses with a collection of his handcrafted bow ties.

20

A Booming Bow-Tie Business

Moziah "Mo" Bridges has always had an extremely strong sense of style. At a young age, his grandma taught him that it is important to "look sharp." Bridges took his grandma's advice seriously and began wearing bow ties. But, he was not satisfied with the bow ties he found in local stores. The colors were too plain and most were clip-ons. He decided to do something about it.

Bridges started Mo's Bows in 2011 when he was just 9 years old. He asked his grandma to teach him how to sew and used his newly acquired sewing skills to make fashionable bow ties. Within a few months, he had over two-dozen bow ties. He started sharing them with his friends and family. They loved them! Bridges knew he had something special. He created a website to sell his product and wrote, "I like to wear bow ties because they make me look good and feel good."

LET'S EXPLORE MATH

This table shows possible numbers of bow ties Bridges makes in five days. Use the information to answer the questions.

Day	1	2	3	4	5
Bow Ties	6	12	18	24	30

1. What pattern do you notice in the numbers of bow ties?
2. If the pattern continues, how many bow ties will he make after 10 days? Explain your thinking.

As word spread about Mo's Bows, Bridges started selling his bow ties through social media and in stores near his home in Memphis, Tennessee. Soon, the orders began flying in. Bridges asked his mom, grandma, and other family members to help him make bow ties and mail the orders. Just two years after starting his company, he had sold 2,000 handmade bow ties. Those sales totaled $55,000!

In 2013, Bridges and his mom were on the show *Shark Tank*. They hoped to get money for the business. Daymond John made a deal to help grow Bridges's business. But, John did not give them money. Instead, he offered to mentor him for free! John is the founder of a successful clothing line called FUBU. So, Bridges agreed to this valuable offer.

John thought that Bridges should add neckties to his line of products. Bridges followed the advice of his mentor. He now makes bow ties, neckties, and pocket squares.

Bridges and his mom appear on *Shark Tank*.

Moziah "Mo" Bridges and Daymond John

HANDCRAFTED

O'S BOWS

BOW TIES

EST.2012

Giving Back and Looking Ahead

Bridges believes it is important to give back to his community. In 2015, he gave $1,600 to send 10 kids from Memphis to summer camp. The kids and their families would not have been able to afford it without his help. Bridges posted on his blog, "Memphis is ranked the highest in child hunger. Most kids only get a meal when school is in session. At the community center, the kids get a meal and playtime. Giving back to my community really helped me feel humble. It also makes me smile because I see other kids smiling and enjoying the camp."

Suppose Bridges sells each adult bow tie for $50. Using this revenue, he puts $35 in a savings account and spends the remaining $15 on business expenses.

1. Complete the table to find how much money he will save and spend after selling 4 bow ties.

2. What patterns do you notice in the dollar amounts? Explain your reasoning.

Bow Ties	Money Saved	Money Spent
1		
2		
3		
4		

What does the future hold for Bridges? In 2015, he signed a deal with Neiman Marcus. Selling through this national chain of stores will help Mo's Bows reach more people. Bridges was also named one of the 30 Most Influential Teens of 2015 by TIME magazine.

But Bridges isn't done yet. He wants to have his own clothing line. He hopes to reach this goal by the time he is 20 years old. He's well on his way!

bicycle shop owner

Changing the World: One Business at a Time

There are certain characteristics that most entrepreneurs have in common. They have creative ideas and visions for the future. They want to work hard and make money. Passion about what they do is a must. They have self-confidence and are not afraid to take risks. Finally, they are open-minded when others offer advice. These are just a few of the many attributes that make business owners successful.

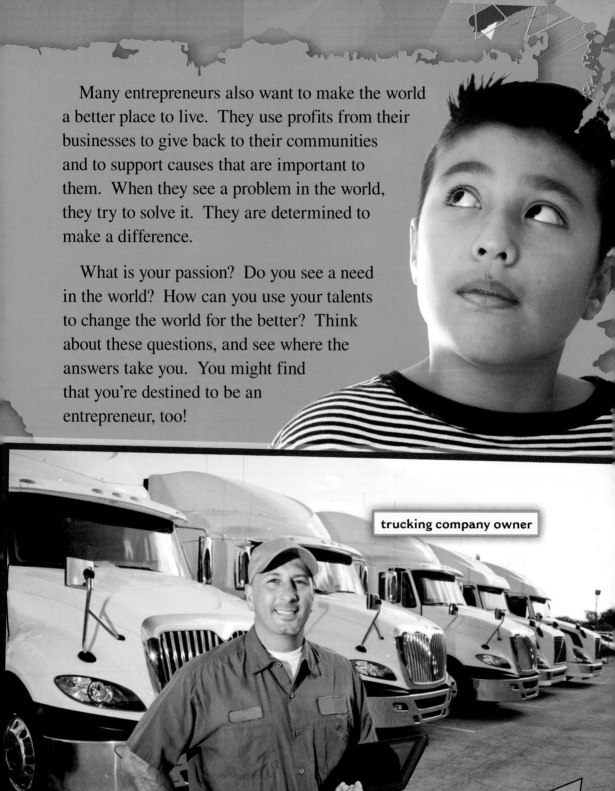

Many entrepreneurs also want to make the world a better place to live. They use profits from their businesses to give back to their communities and to support causes that are important to them. When they see a problem in the world, they try to solve it. They are determined to make a difference.

What is your passion? Do you see a need in the world? How can you use your talents to change the world for the better? Think about these questions, and see where the answers take you. You might find that you're destined to be an entrepreneur, too!

trucking company owner

⚙️ Problem Solving

Keisha loves to make hair bows and headbands for her friends and family. She starts selling them at local craft fairs. Within a few months, she is selling her products on a website. That's when her business really takes off! She even hires a few employees to help keep up with orders. After a few years and lots of hard work, her sales continue to increase.

The table on the right shows her revenue for the first three years. Use the information in the table to answer the questions.

1. Draw a number line and plot the revenue from each year. Then, use the number line to round each amount to the nearest ten thousand dollars.

2. What is Keisha's total estimated revenue from these three years? What is the total exact revenue? How do these amounts compare?

3. Keisha wants to know the approximate differences in revenue amounts from each year to the next. Estimate the differences. Explain how you know.

4. If revenue continues to increase in the same approximate pattern, what can Keisha estimate her sales will be in Year 4?

Keisha's Bows and Headbands

Year	Revenue
1	$10,345
2	$20,098
3	$29,879

Glossary

creative—having the ability to make new things and have new ideas

economics—relating to the system of buying goods and services

employees—people who work for another person or for a company

entrepreneurs—people who start and run their own businesses

expenses—money spent regularly to pay for things

extinct—no longer existing

finances—money available to a person, business, or government

invest—to give money to someone or something to make a profit

mentor—a person who teaches or gives advice based on their experiences

profits—money that is made in a business after all of the costs have been paid

promote—to make people aware of a business or product

resources—supplies

revenue—money that is made by a company

savings—money put aside in an account at a bank

successful—having achieved the desired result

Index

Answer Key

Let's Explore Math

page 7:
$63; Strategies may include subtracting $87 from $150.

page 11:
$6,724; To check, add the expenses and profit to be sure the sum is equal to the revenue.

page 15:
1. $1,000; Example: On the number line, $1,478 is closer to $1,000 than $2,000.

2. $4,000; Example: On the number line, $3,765 is closer to $4,000 than $3,000.

3. $5,000; Example: The estimate is less than the exact total because $1,478 is rounded to $1,000, even though it is very close to $1,500.

page 17:
$1,587; Strategies may include subtracting $1,088 from $2,675

page 21:
1. The number of bow ties increases by 6 each day.

2. 60 bow ties after 10 days; Strategies will vary, but may include continuing the table.

page 25:
1. Saved: $35; $70; $105; $140
   Spent: $15; $30; $45; $60

2. Possible answers: The amounts saved for each bow tie increase by $35; The amounts spent for each bow tie increase by $15.

Problem Solving

1. Year 1: $10,000; Year 2: $20,000; Year 3: $30,000; Number line should show the dollar amounts close to these estimates.

2. $60,000; $60,322; The estimated and exact amounts are close. The exact amount is greater than the estimated amount.

3. The estimated difference between each year is about $10,000. Explanations will vary.

4. Answers will vary, but should be about $40,000.